THE JOY OF SHARING JESUS

Discover

by
Diane and Brent Averill

FAITH
ALIVE®
Christian Resources

Grand Rapids, Michigan

Cover photo: PhotoDisc

Faith Alive Christian Resources published by CRC Publications. Discover Your Bible series. *Discover the Joy of Sharing Jesus,* © 2002 by CRC Publications, 2850 Kalamazoo Ave. SE, Grand Rapids, MI 49560. All rights reserved. With the exception of brief excerpts for review purposes, no part of this book may be reproduced in any manner whatsoever without written permission from the publisher. Printed in the United States of America on recycled paper.

We welcome your comments. Call us at 1-800-333-8300 or e-mail us at editors@faithaliveresources.org.

ISBN 1-56212-860-4

10 9 8 7 6 5 4 3 2 1

Contents

To the Leader

Prepare the Lesson

This leader guide is meant to assist small group leaders, not to substitute for your own personal work. Always answer the study guide questions first, using the suggested basic steps of preparation. Then use the leader material to enrich your understanding of the passage.

Do not take the leader guide to the Bible study group. You do not want to give the impression that you have an answer book. The answers are in the Bible; you are a guide to help your group find the answers in God's Word.

Prepare thoroughly before each group session so that you can lead without frequent references to your notes. This will leave you free to concentrate on your leadership responsibilities. You will also be able to keep better eye contact and listen more carefully.

Get Ready to Lead

Learn to think in questions. As you prepare the lesson, ask yourself questions and discover your own answers. There is no better way to prepare yourself to anticipate the group's questions and help others discover truths from God's Word.

Lead with Questions

Use questions to direct the discussion. Draw out positive contributions with questions. Break down difficult or unclear questions with smaller, concise questions. Respond to wrong answers or problems with questions. If you learn to lead others to the truth by questions, you will be a good Bible discovery leader. The questions in this study are designed to be used with the New International Version of the Bible, but other translations can be used too.

Help to Apply

Gently help group members discover the meaning of God's message for their own lives. Be careful not to be judgmental of those who are not yet applying these truths. It's the Spirit's work to apply God's Word to the hearts of men and women. Tactfully let the group know how the Spirit is applying it in your heart and life. Pray faithfully for the Spirit's work in others.

Keep application low-key. Be careful not to put any personal pressure on group members to apply the truths. Simply try to help group members see that there is a relationship between the Bible and life. Avoid the use of direct pronouns in application. For example, instead of asking, "What does this mean to you?" ask, "What does this mean in our lives?" or instead of asking, "What will you do?" ask, "What action does this passage suggest?"

Leadership Training

If there is more than one group, leaders are strongly encouraged to meet regularly for discussion of the lesson, for prayer, and for mutual support. Every leader should have a copy of the *Coffee Break Evangelism Manual with Director's Handbook*. This book is a basic "how-to" for establishing and leading a Bible discovery group. Reread the book or portions of it periodically and review it at the beginning of each season. *Leading with Love* in the Coffee Break Core Values series is another important tool for leadership development. Leaders will also find it helpful to attend one of the many leadership training workshops offered each year. For more information on materials or training, write to Discover Your Bible, 2850 Kalamazoo Ave. SE, Grand Rapids, Ml 49560 or P.O. Box 5070, STN LCD 1, Burlington, ON L7R 3Y8, or visit www.FaithAliveResources.org.

Introduction

Sharing our faith is a very personal matter. Sometimes we feel that we'll insult or offend our friends if we talk to them about our faith. Or our friends may have misconceptions or negative perspectives about the Bible's message. Perhaps they have never read the Bible or they have no Christian background. In addition, we're afraid that we may not say things just right, so it is easier to clam up about our faith.

Don't worry about getting it right. People are naturally interested in others' personal stories. Simply using gracious, meaningful words to tell of God's grace in our lives goes a long way in communicating the gospel.

You may have been a Christian for many years, or maybe you are new in your faith. Possibly you are not even certain you have yet crossed the line of faith. Wherever you are on your spiritual journey, you will find this study helpful.

This study uses Colossians 4:2-6 as a framework of four essential elements of the Christian faith.

These include

- prayer,
- a dependence on God to open doors,
- characteristics of grace-filled living, and
- how to answer everyone.

The Scripture passages in this study will help us learn how Jesus and the early apostles interacted with people. We will learn how Paul and other early believers communicated their faith. Most importantly, we will learn to heed Peter's command in 1 Peter 3:15: "In your hearts set apart Christ as Lord. Always be prepared to give an answer to everyone who asks you to give the reason for the hope that you have. But do this with gentleness and respect."

Tips for Leading Your Group

As you begin this study, you may want someone from the group to read the Introduction aloud. Ask: **Have you ever felt misunderstood when talking about your faith? If you were asked to share your faith story, would you be able to do so easily?**

Challenge your group to take time in the coming week to develop a three-minute explanation of how they came to believe in Jesus Christ. Those who were raised in a Christian home may say they have no story to tell. The opposite is the case. Their story would simply be more like Timothy's testimony (2 Tim. 1) than Paul's (Acts 9, 22, and 26). If they cannot name a specific date when they first trusted Christ, ask them to think of an event when they knew for certain that Christ was their personal Savior.

Be sensitive to group members who have not yet come to faith. They may be hearing the gospel for the first time in this study. Be sure to use language that they will understand. Look for natural opportunities to speak with them and to answer their questions. It can be as simple as going out for coffee and asking them what they think of the study or how their understanding of Jesus has changed. To make sure they feel included as participants, you may want to assign them the task of asking a Christian they know to tell how he or she came to believe in Christ.

As you prepare each lesson, think of how you would approach it if you were a nonbeliever. Ask yourself what might be confusing or difficult. Remember that you may have the opportunity to put into practice the principles you learn. Pray that the Holy Spirit will give you the right words to say to everyone in your group.

Glossary of Terms

Acts—a term used to describe the historical events (acts) of several apostles, especially Peter and Paul, in the early period of the Christian church. A physician named Luke wrote the narrative commonly called the Acts of the Apostles.

apostle—another word for one of the twelve disciples who were commissioned, or sent out, by Christ to proclaim the gospel. Christ also appointed Paul an apostle.

clear conscience—having no personal "baggage" to hide from others; living free of sinful patterns that would discredit what you say.

Colosse—a city located in present-day Turkey (near Laodicea) where Christianity took root. There is no evidence that Paul visited the place. Paul's letter to the church there is called the epistle to the Colossians.

Corinthians—residents of the city of Corinth, the primary commercial center and capital of the Greek province Achaia. Paul's letters 1 and 2 Corinthians are directed to the Christian church he established there.

devote—commit oneself to live a life of wholehearted service to Christ and his teachings.

Ephesus—a seaport city and significant commercial center located in present-day western Turkey. The apostle Paul spent a significant amount of time in this city, and an important Christian community developed there. Paul also wrote a letter to the church in Ephesus called the epistle to the Ephesians.

Galatians—residents of Galatia, a province in present-day north central Turkey. The Galatian believers were reverting to a form of legalism when Paul sent his corrective letter to them.

glorious inheritance—a place in heaven or glory, which Christians will receive when they die.

gospel—literally means "good news." The gospel is the message that God's Son, Jesus Christ, took the punishment for our sins upon himself, dying on the cross, and rose again for the salvation of his people; that he ascended into heaven; and that he will someday return to fully establish his kingdom.

Jacob—grandson of Abraham; he had twelve sons whose descendants became the twelve tribes of ancient Israel.

John—a disciple of Jesus who wrote one of the four gospel accounts in the New Testament. He was a close personal friend of Jesus and an eyewitness to Jesus' life. He also wrote several New Testament letters and the book of Revelation.

mystery of Christ—the surprising meaning of God's eternal plan for all people, revealed to us through the person and work of Jesus Christ.

outsiders—people who do not believe in Jesus Christ, or who are outside the Christian faith.

Paul—a highly educated and religious Jew who initially rejected Christianity but came to faith after a miraculous encounter with Jesus. Paul played a key role in the founding of the early church; he wrote many of the letters in the New Testament.

Philippi—a seaport city located in present-day Greece. The apostle Paul established the church there and wrote the people a letter called the epistle to the Philippians.

proclaim—to make known the good news of God's grace and the forgiveness of sins.

saint—a person who trusts Jesus as Savior through the power of the Holy Spirit in his or her life.

salt—a mineral used to preserve food or enhance the flavor of food.

Samaria—a small country located between Galilee and Judea. Samaria was inhabited primarily by the descendants of the ten northern tribes of Israel who were carried off into captivity but who returned to their homeland and married foreigners. The Samaritans were considered to be a mixed race and not truly Jewish. Jews considered them enemies and heretics and refused to have any contact with them.

Silas—an apostle who worked with Paul and accompanied him on some of his missionary trips.

sinner—one who disobeys God's law as revealed in human conscience and God's Word, the Bible.

Sychar—one of the chief Samaritan cities located near Mount Gerazim. It was the place where Jacob dug a well nearly two thousand years before Christ lived.

Timothy—a follower of Christ and a young protege of Paul who accompanied him on his missionary trips.

Thessalonians—residents of Thessalonica, a seaport city in northern Greece. Paul established a church in this city and wrote two letters to the church there.

Lesson 1

Colossians 4:2-4; Ephesians 6:19; Philippians 4:6;
Acts 2:42-47; Ephesians 1:18-20; John 17:20-23

Prayer: The Essential Ingredient

Introductory Notes

Mike was about the last person you would expect to trust Jesus. He made it clear to any Christians he met that he wanted nothing to do with anything religious. Mike was convinced that he did not need God, and his spicy language reinforced his conviction. He was willing to concede, though, that his wife needed God and the church. When Mike's wife came to faith, her church community began to pray for the impossible: Mike's salvation. After six months of concentrated and intentional prayer, someone from the church shared the gospel and Mike prayed for salvation. It was a miracle. But Mike had seen the change in his wife's life, and he had observed the kindness of the church. Mike is a reminder that God does indeed answer "impossible" prayers.

This lesson will cover passages of Scripture that remind us that prayer is essential to sharing our faith. We need to ask for God's guidance and follow God's leading.

Optional Opening Share Question

What are some ways people communicate with God?

Allow a few minutes for group members to share experiences they have had with prayer. **Did you feel that God was speaking to you? Was it a positive or negative experience?** Be sure to accept each answer. Don't get bogged down with the theological implications of each answer. If an answer sounds questionable, simply say "That's interesting" and move on.

Encourage your group to think of prayer as a two-way conversation. We pray not only for the people we know who are open to the gospel, but also for God to lead us to people to whom we should speak. It is important that we not do all the talking in our prayer conversations with God. Rather, we should tune our ears to hear God's voice in these matters. Listen carefully to your group's comments. Be especially aware of those who may be struggling spiritually. Your goal is to help them see prayer as two-way communication.

1. *Colossians 4:2-4*

   ²Devote yourselves to prayer, being watchful and thankful. ³And pray for us, too, that God may open a door for our message, so that we may proclaim the mystery of Christ, for which I am in chains. ⁴Pray that I may proclaim it clearly, as I should.

   Note: Paul was put in prison simply to await a trial or hearing or even to appease those who falsely accused him of disturbing the peace. He was not guilty of criminal activity.

   a. *What does it mean to be devoted to prayer?*

   It means to make prayer a priority in one's life. Prayer is not an option for the Christian; it is a prerequisite to sharing one's faith. **What things are people devoted to today? Children? Spouse? Jobs? How does being watchful and thankful capture the essence of prayerful preparation?** The word for *watchful* is translated "be wide awake" elsewhere in the New Testament. Jesus used the word in Matthew 26:38ff. when he asked his disciples to watch and pray before Judas Iscariot betrayed him. The disciples had fallen asleep, so being watchful meant to be awake and alert in prayer. **How might this insight help you as you prepare to talk with someone about your faith? Why should we be watchful? How will a thankful attitude affect the way we talk about our faith?**

   b. *What specific things does Paul want people to pray for? Why?*

   Paul wants people to pray that God would open doors so that he could share his faith with others. **What is our part in opening a door?** Remember that God often uses people, but never forget that it is God's power and not our cleverness that opens the door to others. Paul also wants people to pray that he would proclaim the gospel clearly so that people can understand it. Presenting a simple, understandable message about our experience with Jesus is an essential component of sharing our faith. The message must be clear and uncluttered.

   How can we avoid presenting an unclear message? Our prayer is that we will be able to speak sensibly with people and to understand their spiritual situation. This is only possible when the Holy Spirit works in their lives and ours.

   c. *Why does Paul want others to pray for him?*

   Paul knows that God is the one who will open doors for the proclamation of the gospel. Knowing that others are praying will give him the confidence for the task. **Is prayer more effective when more than one person is praying? How can we follow Paul's example?**

In your discussion suggest that group members ask a small group of friends to pray specifically for their attempts to share their faith. If you are leading a grow group, have members suggest ways they can support each other in prayer. Incidentally, even newcomers can see the value of having friends pray for them.

2. **Ephesians 6:19**

> Pray also for me, that whenever I open my mouth, words may be given me so that I will fearlessly make known the mystery of the gospel.

   a. *What request does Paul make of the Ephesian Christians?*

Paul wants God to give him the words to speak, and he wants to be able to speak without fear. While it is true that God gives people insight into the needs of others, we also must be prepared to present a very clear message.

Jesus promised that in difficult circumstances he would give his followers the words to speak. The apostle Paul taught that the Spirit himself gives believers the words to say. Your grow group may wish to turn to 1 Corinthians 2:13ff. and discuss this concept. (See also Moses' complaint and the Lord's answer in Ex. 4:10-12.)

   b. *What difference does it make if people are praying for us?*

Are you ever fearful when you talk to others about your beliefs? What is it that you fear? Do you fear that you will fail to unlock the "mystery of Christ"? (See the glossary.) How will the knowledge that others are praying for you help you open your mouth? How might we hold each other accountable in this regard? **The fact that we know others are praying for us should provide confidence as well as the realization that we are not alone in our effort.**

3. **Philippians 4:6**

> Do not be anxious about anything, but in everything, by prayer and petition, with thanksgiving, present your requests to God.

   Note: A petition is a request and is normally understood to be one element of prayer.

   a. *What is the antidote to fear and anxiety?*

The passage teaches that the antidote is prayer to God about our concerns and fears. **What are some anxieties we have when we speak with others? How is it a comfort to know that the one who is all-powerful hears our prayers? Why would this make us thankful?** God is the one who opens doors and helps us to walk through them. Furthermore, God promises to give us help and confidence so that our words will have a meaningful impact.

b.   Why is this prayer request important?

It is important because we fear rejection. This is one of the greatest fears people have in interpersonal relationships. Rejection stifles our ability to speak to others. It makes us even more hesitant to share our faith. **How would our prayer give us confidence?** Our fear can be overcome when we articulate our fears in prayer. In response, God strengthens us and gives us a greater resolve to share our faith with others. As with many situations in life, the more we do something, the more natural it becomes. Often one difficult experience keeps us from speaking with others. However, when we discover that people are genuinely interested in what we have to say, we will become more comfortable in speaking about our faith.

4.   Acts 2:42-47

⁴²They devoted themselves to the apostles' teaching and to the fellowship, to the breaking of bread and to prayer. ⁴³Everyone was filled with awe, and many wonders and miraculous signs were done by the apostles. ⁴⁴All the believers were together and had everything in common. ⁴⁵Selling their possessions and goods, they gave to anyone as he had need. ⁴⁶Every day they continued to meet together in the temple courts. They broke bread in their homes and ate together with glad and sincere hearts, ⁴⁷praising God and enjoying the favor of all the people. And the Lord added to their number daily those who were being saved.

a.   What happened when the early church devoted itself to fellowship and prayer?

Great things happened to the group and to individuals as well. They developed unity as their mutual appreciation of God was reinforced. They helped each other and found genuine fulfillment in their lives. Most significantly, God added to their numbers, because the spirit of prayer and learning was infectious. **Have you ever known someone with an infectious faith? What was this person like? How can we have an infectious faith? What needs of others might we be in a position to meet?** Be sure not to limit your answers to material needs. Although there is significant material need in our society, there are other needs as well. People today often need to know that someone is interested in them. They need role models for their relationships. Time is valuable; when we spend time with people, it shows them that we care. **How does sharing our beliefs translate into action?**

b.   How often did people come to faith?

The early church was so activated by prayer and sharing that people came to faith on a daily basis.

c. Is this the norm in the church today? Why or why not?

The church today, with some exceptions, seems far removed from the experience of the early church. Take a few minutes to discuss why this appears to be the case. If you are leading a grow group, ask: **How can a sharing and caring community be a source of encouragement today?** Remember that in the early church there was a strong emphasis on relationships. As you discuss these matters, be aware that some group members may have negative comments to offer about a certain church. Be ready to turn the discussion in a more positive direction. All members of a local church should desire it to become what God wants it to be, and work toward that goal. **What can Christians today do to restore the New Testament perspective of community?**

5. *Ephesians 1:18-20*

    [18]I pray also that the eyes of your heart may be enlightened in order that you may know the hope to which he has called you, the riches of his glorious inheritance in the saints, [19]and his incomparably great power for us who believe. That power is like the working of his mighty strength, [20]which he exerted in Christ when he raised him from the dead and seated him at his right hand in the heavenly realms.

    a. What is the first thing Paul prays for in verse 18? How is this accomplished?

Paul prays that his readers might have their minds open to the great hope that each of them has in heaven, because this hope is a powerful incentive. The phrase "eyes of your heart" suggests a continual vision of enlightenment from the Holy Spirit. Overall, verse 18 gives us a glimpse of the believer's future as a child of God. **How does a hope of eternal life change our perspective now?**

Now that you've touched on the topic of eternal life, you might want to ask if group members have saving faith. Be careful though. Since this is your first meeting together, ask only if you feel group members would not be unduly put off by the question. You might ask, "If you were to die tonight and God were to ask you, 'Why should I let you into heaven?' what would you say?"

People who have not yet trusted Christ may mention the good life they have led or the good works they have done. Explain that Christianity is a matter of *done* rather than *do*. It is based on what Christ has done for us by dying on the cross, rather than on the good works we might do for him. Good works are an indication that we have true faith; they are done out of gratitude for our salvation. We might say good works come after salvation, not before. Be sensitive to group members who may be struggling with this concept. You may need to limit the discussion and offer to speak to anyone with questions after the session has ended.

> b. *What kind of power is available to those who believe in Christ? Why is this power important?*

This power is the same power God exercised when God raised Christ from the dead and restored him to his position of heavenly authority. **How does this thought encourage us? Have you ever felt this kind of power? Do you have it now?** How wonderful that this power is available to all believers. When we share our faith, it is God's power that saves, not the effectiveness of our presentation.

6. *John 17:20-23*

> [20]"My prayer is not for them alone. I pray also for those who will believe in me through their message, [21]that all of them may be one, Father, just as you are in me and I am in you. May they also be in us so that the world may believe that you have sent me. [22]I have given them the glory that you gave me, that they may be one as we are one: [23]I in them and you in me. May they be brought to complete unity to let the world know that you sent me and have loved them even as you have loved me."

> a. *For whom is Jesus praying? What does he ask?*

Jesus is praying for both present and future believers. His prayer is a request for unity. The purpose of this unity is not simply for the sake of believers; it is also a mark of God's presence that speaks to people who have yet to believe. **What things can we do to indicate our unity with other Christians? How does disunity diminish the Christian message?**

> b. *What encouragement and challenge should this knowledge give us?*

We should be encouraged with the knowledge that Jesus is praying for us today. His prayer empowers us to be witnesses of God's love and grace to the world.

7. *Summary*

How will this lesson help us if we come across people like Mike in our life?

It will help to review the essential elements of prayer in the passages of this lesson, especially those that teach that divine power is unleashed by the prayers of the saints. Then we will know how to speak with people and they will be prepared by God to hear the message.

Lesson 2

Colossians 4:3; 1 Thessalonians 2:6b-13; Galatians 6:9;
Philippians 2:3-8

Open Doors

Introductory Notes

Joe was a single dad whose wife had left him with three small children. His Christian next-door neighbors befriended him. They helped encourage him in countless ways—bringing meals, babysitting, and providing a listening ear. As helpful as their relationship was, the neighbors knew Joe and his children needed a relationship with God through Jesus Christ.

They began to talk with him about his faith and soon invited him to their church. By the time Joe came to church, he was very open to hearing the gospel message about Jesus Christ. His neighbors had consistently modeled Christlike compassion and love.

This lesson touches on how we can encourage openness in the people we contact. The first step is to build a trusting relationship. Christians are often viewed with suspicion, so our lives must not hinder the message we bring. Christ is our ultimate example as we seek to show his love to others. We cannot expect people to be open to our words if we have failed to open our hearts and lives to them first.

Optional Opening Share Question

Discuss a time when you felt very welcome. What contributed to this feeling?

Most group members should be able to think of such a time. Maybe when they went to a new school for the first time and another child befriended them. Or maybe when a neighbor arrived with a welcome gift after they moved into a new home. Note that we look for open doors not because we view people as projects, but because we never want to get in the way of Christ. We don't want to hinder the gospel message by our actions or attitudes. This does not mean that we should pretend to be perfect. We know that we fall short of that standard. However, our lives must confirm our message. Lee Strobel, a former atheist who came to faith because of his neighbor's witness, says that he knew his neighbors were not perfect but their actions were genuine.

1. *Colossians 4:3*

    And pray for us, too, that God may open a door for our message, so that we may proclaim the mystery of Christ, for which I am in chains.

    Note: Paul was imprisoned—"in chains"—for his faith when he wrote this letter. "Us" (v. 3) refers to the individuals who were with Paul at the time. Several are mentioned in Colossians 4.

    a. *What does Paul's "open door" image suggest?*

    Paul is teaching that God provides opportunities for believers to enter people's lives. He prays that God will allow him to present the gospel in a compelling way. **When have you experienced an "open door" in your life? Have you ever experienced a "closed door"?** Group members may think of examples from their careers or education when they were "at the right place at the right time."

    Encourage group members also to think of their experiences when God seemed to be opening doors to share their faith with others. Note that Paul also refers to open doors in 1 Corinthians 16:9 and 2 Corinthians 2:12.

    b. *What will hinder doors from being opened?*

    If God decides to open a door, then it will be opened. However, things like our lack of prayer or study or faith can hinder the doors from being opened. Perhaps the greatest hindrance is insensitivity. Paul followed Jesus' example and approached people with compassion and sensitivity. **If someone cautiously opens a door a crack, how do we encourage him or her to open it a little more?** Perhaps by putting the person at ease. **How can Christians become more sensitive to people who have not yet come to faith?**

2. *1 Thessalonians 2:6b-12*

    ⁶ᵇAs apostles of Christ we could have been a burden to you, ⁷but we were gentle among you, like a mother caring for her little children. ⁸We loved you so much that we were delighted to share with you not only the gospel of God but our lives as well, because you had become so dear to us. ⁹Surely you remember, brothers, our toil and hardship; we worked night and day in order not to be a burden to anyone while we preached the gospel of God to you.

    ¹⁰You are witnesses, and so is God, of how holy, righteous and blameless we were among you who believed. ¹¹For you know that we dealt with each of you as a father deals with his own children, ¹²encouraging, comforting and urging you to live lives worthy of God, who calls you into his kingdom and glory.

    Note: When Paul uses the term *we*, he may be including his companions Silas and Timothy.

a. *Why would Paul use the family image to describe his relationship with the Thessalonians?*

Family relationships have always been a vital building block of society. Paul here tells the Thessalonian believers that he views his relationship with them in terms of a healthy family. Those who respond to God's message are included in God's family. They need to be treated as such. **What does it mean to treat others "like family"? What words describe healthy family relationships? How can this approach open more doors?** Group members may suggest words like *loving, tender, listening, understanding, empathy.* Obviously, we must have the same kind of attitude toward those who are not yet members of the family of God.

b. *What can we learn from Paul's relationship with the Thessalonian believers?*

Paul had earned the right to share what he believed because he had lived with the Thessalonians for a time as well. **How would you describe Paul's relationship with the Thessalonian believers? What was Paul delighted to do? Why do you think he was delighted to do this?** Paul told the Thessalonians that he and his friends had lived exemplary lives among them. **Do we need to live perfect lives in order to have credibility with others? What positive impact on others does Christian living have? Does honesty about our shortcomings diminish or enhance our message? Why or why not?** If you are leading a grow group, you may want to take a few extra minutes with these questions.

c. *Describe Paul's effort to reach people.*

Today we would say that Paul was giving "110 percent" as he reached out to the Thessalonians with love and care. **How might such an effort affect the way we live? Would this approach require a shift in our priorities?** Take a few minutes to make this discussion as practical as possible. The requirement for us is no different than it was for Paul. Some group members may feel that they don't have adequate time or energy to devote to this effort. Of course, we all are busy people, and Paul was a full-time missionary. We can't expect to be in such a relationship with dozens of people. Help your group members understand that it's OK if we have such a caring relationship only with one or two people at a time. When we are dealing with people, quality is more important than quantity.

3. *1 Thessalonians 2:13*

And we also thank God continually because, when you received the word of God, which you heard from us, you accepted it not as the word of men, but as it actually is, the word of God, which is at work in you who believe.

a. What is the ultimate source of our message?

The ultimate source of our message is God as found in the pages of Scripture. It therefore is a consistently activating and challenging message. **What difference does it make that our message is from God's inspired Word?** When we speak with people, we should make it clear that our message comes from the Bible and not from our own thinking. In fact, showing them a passage in the Bible will help them to see the actual source. This is also a way to encourage people to look at the Bible for themselves.

Why is it important to indicate the source of our message? It is important because our message does not simply evolve from human wisdom. For example, Jesus' claim to be God is not simply a matter of our own opinion; it is a claim that Jesus made for himself. To disagree with this truth is to disagree with Jesus himself. Many people today think the Bible is no different than any other religious book. Some of your group members may have questions about the trustworthiness, accuracy, or authority of the Bible. If such questions are raised, suggest that group members read *Hard Questions People Ask About the Christian Faith* by Case Van Kempen (Faith Alive, 2002, 1-800-333-8300) or *Questions of Life* by Nicky Gumbel (David C. Cook, 1996). Of course, be sure to offer to talk with them further about their questions at another time.

4. Galatians 6:9

Let us not become weary in doing good, for at the proper time we will reap a harvest if we do not give up.

a. What does "doing good" mean?

Encourage your group members to be as specific as possible with their answers. If appropriate, have them think through (or even open) their daytimers or appointment books. **What entries would they place under the heading "Doing Good"?** Generally, "doing good" includes doing good works and making daily choices that are consistent with the Christian faith. **What does a life of "doing good" look like to other people? Is it a life of rules and regulations or a life of kindness and compassion? Explain. Why might Paul suggest that weariness is also a part of this life?** Paul recognizes that investing time and energy in other people is often a long-term commitment. It is only human nature to experience a certain level of fatigue even when our actions and motivations are godly.

b.   How do we keep from becoming weary in "doing good"?

We must take time for spiritual refreshment. **How might we do this?** Jesus went on a personal retreat to be alone with God. He encouraged his disciples to do the same. If we would be effective witnesses, we must take time to pray and to be renewed by God. If you are leading a grow group, discuss ways in which people can be energized in their faith walk. Ask group members to share specific times they have experienced such refreshment. *Note:* The harvest in this text refers to believers' receiving the reward of eternal life.

5.   *Philippians 2:3-4*

³Do nothing out of selfish ambition or vain conceit, but in humility consider others better than yourselves. ⁴Each of you should look not only to your own interests, but also to the interests of others.

a.   How do "selfish ambition" and "vain conceit" close doors?

What does Paul mean by "selfish ambition" and "vain conceit"? What does that look like today? How does a selfish, conceited person act or talk? Group members should have no trouble identifying with Paul's command. We all know people who have highly inflated impressions of themselves. Paul, however, takes us to the other end of the spectrum: humility.

Humility is the most effective way to reach people who have yet to believe in Christ. **Why is humility so effective?** No one likes to associate with pompous and arrogant people. Our sufficiency is not in ourselves, but in Christ. So we must take a humble approach and communicate our complete dependence on God and his love for the world. **What can we do to communicate sincere humility? How can we avoid sounding condescending?**

b.   How should we view other people?

We view them the same way Jesus and Paul did. After all, people are made in God's image (Gen. 1:27) and are therefore significant in God's eyes. **How do we place other people's interests ahead of our own? Is this a realistic approach today?** As you discuss these questions, be sure to note again that we must not view people as "projects." Rather we must treat others as we would like to be treated. If you are leading a grow group, take a few minutes to discuss the implications of humans being "imagebearers" of God.

6.   *Philippians 2:5-8*

⁵Your attitude should be the same as that of Christ Jesus:
⁶Who, being in very nature God,
did not consider equality with God something to be grasped,
⁷but made himself nothing,

taking the very nature of a servant,
being made in human likeness.
⁸And being found in appearance as a man,
he humbled himself
and became obedient to death—
even death on a cross!

a.   *How do these verses picture Jesus?*

Jesus is pictured here as genuinely humble and obedient to the Father's will. **Was Jesus' humility forced upon him or did he willingly assume it?** It is obvious from this passage that Jesus gave up his heavenly status to become a human servant. Note the phrases "made himself nothing" and "taking the very nature of a servant" and "he humbled himself." These teach clearly that Jesus was not coerced into a state of humility. **What did this act cost him?** Jesus' obedience cost him a great deal, including death on the cross where God's wrath against the sin of all humankind was poured out on Jesus (Isa. 53:4-6).

b.   *What does Jesus' example teach us?*

Jesus' example of humility, service, and obedience is the best way to approach people. This is how Jesus and his disciples approached people. **Why is this way of humility so difficult to achieve in our day? Is humility viewed as a sign of weakness or strength? Explain. What is true humility?** True humility involves knowing who we are in Christ—sinners redeemed by the blood of Jesus Christ. We can never say that we have arrived spiritually. We always view others as imagebearers of God, no matter how distorted that image may be.

7. **Summary**
    What kind of attitude and actions does God use to open doors?

God expects his followers to be fully committed to the Scriptures and to a life of service to others.

The Scriptures in this lesson may have convicted some of your group members concerning ways in which they fail to exhibit such attitudes and actions. If you sense that some members are struggling, take a few minutes for silent prayer and reflection. You might close with a simple prayer of commitment and rededication to "live a life worthy of the calling you have received" (Eph. 4:1-2).

Lesson 3

Colossians 4:5-6; John 4:4-10; 1 Timothy 1:15-16;
2 Corinthians 2:14-17; 1 Peter 3:15-16

Living a Grace-full Life

Introductory Notes

The women of a Bible study group had been praying for other women to come and join their group, especially those who needed to hear about Christ's offer of salvation.

Meanwhile, thousands of miles away, a man was praying for his sister, Tina, who lived in the community where the Bible study met. He had become a Christian and wanted his sister to find faith in Christ as well. He wrote to his sister and encouraged her to join a Bible study.

Soon after receiving the letter, Tina saw an ad in the newspaper for a women's Bible study. The ad seemed warm and inviting. When she called for information, she spoke with a woman who graciously assured her that even if she had never studied the Bible before, she would be more than welcome to attend. When Tina finally came to the Bible study, she found other women who were also kind and welcoming. One in particular— Helen—spent a lot of time with Tina and politely answered her questions. No question was too foolish, and if a question was difficult, they looked for the answer together.

After several weeks, Helen explained the gospel to Tina. Because God had been preparing her heart, Tina readily accepted the truth of what she heard. Helen went on to disciple Tina and eventually Tina's husband came to faith as well. She readily admits that it was the gracious behavior of Christians that drew her to the study in the first place. Their interest in her as a person initially attracted her; that same interest kept her coming back and helped her find faith. This lesson will show from Scripture how we can be grace-full as we approach others with a grace-full message from God.

Optional Opening Share Question

Describe an experience of being treated either in a gracious or an ungracious manner.

Help your group members discuss their experiences. **What did the experience feel like? What did they learn from it?** Think of how an unbeliever would respond in a similar situation. **What might help or hinder you from listening to someone?** If any of your group members shares an ungracious experience, be sure not to dwell on the negative perspective. Encourage someone in the group to share a positive experience.

1. Colossians 4:5-6

⁵Be wise in the way you act toward outsiders; make the most of every opportunity. ⁶Let your conversation be always full of grace, seasoned with salt, so that you may know how to answer everyone.

a. What does a grace-filled conversation sound like?

A grace-filled conversation is one in which the speaker states positive and constructive things. Critical and judgmental words are not part of this speech. Critical people think and speak critically without giving it a second thought. Their approach is often ingrained. On the other hand, grace-filled conversations build up the listener. They do not tear down the person. Believers need to speak graciously in private as well as in public and must speak to everyone in a grace-filled way. For example, how would you feel if the grocery clerk you snapped at this morning showed up at your Bible study this afternoon? If you are leading a grow group, ask, **What does it mean to "speak the truth in love" (Eph. 4:15)? Is it the responsibility of believers to correct wrong behavior of others, particularly of those who have not yet become believers? Why or why not? Is it possible to damage relationships when we try to do the Holy Spirit's work? Explain.** You might also talk about paying "relational rent," that is, earning the right to speak with people about spiritual things by spending relational time with them. It is also important to remember to ask questions graciously rather than to jump to conclusions.

b. Salt can either enhance the flavor of food or preserve it. Explain what the phrase "seasoned with salt" might imply.

The phrase "seasoned with salt" could have various meanings. Since salt was used as a preservative, it may mean that our speech should be free from corruption. The metaphor further suggests that our conversations with others should be appropriate to the context and fitting to our hearers. Our conversations should be flavored so as not to be too bland or too spicy. They should have life and energy. If you are leading a grow group, read Ephesians 4:29 and ask, **What does it mean to "build others up" and "benefit those who listen"? How do we speak with people so that they genuinely benefit from what we say?**

24

2. *John 4:4-10*

[4]Now [Jesus] had to go through Samaria. [5]So he came to a town in Samaria called Sychar, near the plot of ground Jacob had given to his son Joseph. [6]Jacob's well was there, and Jesus, tired as he was from the journey, sat down by the well. It was about the sixth hour.

[7]When a Samaritan woman came to draw water, Jesus said to her, "Will you give me a drink?" [8](His disciples had gone into the town to buy food.)

[9]The Samaritan woman said to him, "You are a Jew and I am a Samaritan woman. How can you ask me for a drink?" (For Jews do not associate with Samaritans.)

[10]Jesus answered her, "If you knew the gift of God and who it is that asks you for a drink, you would have asked him and he would have given you living water."

a.   What was it about Jesus that surprised the woman?

She was surprised about a number of things. First, she was surprised that as a man, he spoke to a woman. Second, she was surprised that as a Jew, he would speak to a Samaritan. **Since this was uncommon in that day, do you think Jesus deliberately set up this encounter? Why?**

b.   How did Jesus capture her attention?

Jesus piqued her interest about water and indicated that he could supply living water. **Why was Jesus' question about water so appropriate in this situation? In what way did he stir up her interest?** The Samaritan woman probably had not given much thought to her daily task of drawing water. Jesus, however, used the elements of his encounter with her to grab her attention. His words about "living water" surely were new.

c.   What can we learn from Jesus' encounter with this woman?

Jesus asked the woman to do something she was able to do (draw water), and he did it in a gracious and intriguing way. **Did he challenge the customs of his day to speak with her? Did he approach her first? What does this tell us about waiting for people to come to us?** Be sure that your group understands that sometimes we need to go to people, rather than expecting them to come to us. Encourage your group to think about ways they could reach out to people today. If you are leading a grow group ask, **Why do believers so often isolate themselves?** This was not Jesus' practice. He went to the place of need. **Where can we go to meet people who need Jesus? What club or organization might we join that would put us in touch with people who are not part of a faith community?** Take a few minutes with these questions of application. You may want to ask group members to write down how they will rearrange their schedule to meet people.

3. *1 Timothy 1:15-16*

> [15]Here is a trustworthy saying that deserves full acceptance: Christ Jesus came into the world to save sinners—of whom I am the worst. [16]But for that very reason I was shown mercy so that in me, the worst of sinners, Christ Jesus might display his unlimited patience as an example for those who would believe on him and receive eternal life.

    a.   *How did Paul view himself? Why?*

Paul viewed himself in an honest and objective way. He said that he was the worst of sinners. **Do you think he was referring only to the time before he was a believer?** Notice the tense of the verb—"I am." He was referring to his sinful condition the very day he penned those words. In comparison to God's perfect standard, he knew he fell far short. Nothing would be gained by comparing himself with other people, and his only concern was to point out that Christ came into the world to save people like himself. **How would this truth keep him humble?**

    b.   *What impact might Paul's example have on people today?*

It is difficult to admit that we might be the "worst of sinners." **Why is that so?** Such an evaluation does not mean that we are as bad as we possibly can be. It does mean, however, that we fall far short in our attitudes and actions before a perfect and holy God. If we believe this to be true about ourselves, we should be able to relate to others in true humility. In turn, they will be more likely to listen to our message. As one writer puts it, "We are all beggars telling other beggars where to find food." If you are leading a grow group, ask, **How do nonbelieving people view Christians? Why are Christians sometimes viewed as arrogant and judgmental?**

4. *2 Corinthians 2:14-16a*

> [14]But thanks be to God, who always leads us in triumphal procession in Christ and through us spreads everywhere the fragrance of the knowledge of him. [15]For we are to God the aroma of Christ among those who are being saved and those who are perishing. [16a]To the one we are the smell of death; to the other, the fragrance of life.

    a.   *Who spreads the fragrance of Christ in the world?*

Notice that God spreads Christ's fragrance through us. **How would you describe that fragrance? What are its characteristics? In what way might it be a pleasing fragrance? Why is it important that we spread the fragrance of Christ and not the fragrance of ourselves? What is the difference?** Note that some people will refuse to believe. To them, our message will be the smell of death rather than the fragrance of life. **What does the "smell of** death" suggest? What are its characteristics? How dramatic or overpowering is that smell?** As you guide this discussion, be sure to distinguish between the *message* we present and our *manner* of presentation. We must be careful not to "smell bad" in our presentation of the message.

b.   *What does this imagery imply?*

Commentator Philip Hughes notes that triumphal processions in Paul's day were accompanied by the odor of burning spices in the streets (*A Commentary on the Epistle to the Hebrews*, Eerdmans, 1977). **Who walks in this triumphal procession? Who sees it?** We need to make a positive, gracious impression on people. They are watching us. Therefore, we need to be attractive in our approach to others.

5.   *2 Corinthians 2:16b-17*

   16b And who is equal to such a task? 17Unlike so many, we do not peddle the word of God for profit. On the contrary, in Christ we speak before God with sincerity, like men sent from God.

a.   *What does Paul's question (v. 16b) suggest?*

None of us can do this in our own strength, but in Christ and with his strength we are equipped to spread the fragrance of Christ. **How do we tap into this strength?** If you are leading a grow group, read 2 Corinthians 3:5, where Paul identifies the source of our competency.

b.   *How do we speak "with sincerity" before God and people?*

We speak "with sincerity" when we come to people with no ulterior motives other than a desire to see them respond to Jesus in faith. We do not do it for profit or personal gain. **What might be some insincere motives in sharing our faith? Can you think of people who "peddle the word of God for profit" today?** Your group members may mention the name of some televangelist or radio preacher. While it is tempting to point fingers at others, don't allow your group to stray from the context of the passage. It is God who supplies all we need as we share our faith with others. In a grow group you might ask, **How do we avoid viewing unbelievers as trophies to boast about or projects to work on?**

6.   *1 Peter 3:15-16*

   15But in your hearts set apart Christ as Lord. Always be prepared to give an answer to everyone who asks you to give the reason for the hope that you have. But do this with gentleness and respect, 16keeping a clear conscience, so that those who speak maliciously against your good behavior in Christ may be ashamed of their slander.

a.   What should be our attitude when we share our faith?

We must be gentle and kind; we also must respect those we are speaking with. **How can we be gentle and respectful of people who disagree with us?** Remember that treating people respectfully has the potential of bearing fruit later on. Sometimes people disagree for the sole purpose of seeing how we will respond to their disagreement. If we project a gracious attitude, it will be more difficult for them to dismiss our message. In a grow group you might ask, **What factors make it difficult to speak the truth in a gentle and respectful way? Should we ever "water down" the truth in order to be gentle with others?**

b.   Why is a clear conscience necessary? What will be the result?

Having a clear conscience means that you have no personal "baggage" to hide from others. You are who you say you are, living free from any sinful patterns that would discredit what you say. **What is so bad about hypocrisy? How does an inconsistent life harm your message?** If you live a consistent life, those who try to discredit your message with malicious lies and slander will be put to shame. Remember that we do not pretend to be perfect, but we must strive to live lives that are consistent with biblical teaching. If you are leading a grow group, ask, **Why is it difficult for Christians to admit that they are not perfect?**

7.   Summary

What are the key building blocks to a grace-full life?

Have your group members review the Scripture passages in this lesson. You may want to have a whiteboard or large pad of paper ready to list the building blocks suggested by group members. They might include the following:

- conversation that is appropriate and nonjudgmental
- going where the need is
- taking advantage of God-given opportunities
- having a humble attitude
- carrying the fragrance of Christ wherever we go
- speaking with sincerity and respect
- maintaining a clear conscience

If we understand that the grace we have received has come to us through Christ alone, we will be gracious to everyone we meet.

Lesson 4

Colossians 4:5-6; Acts 17:22-34; 1 Corinthians 9:19-22;
2 Corinthians 4:1-4

Ready to Give an Answer

Introductory Notes

Kayo's American husband brought her to the United States before he left for a tour of duty with the navy. Kayo was a long way from her home in Japan. She knew no one but was anxious to learn about her husband's country. Kayo thought she could learn something about his culture by attending a church nearby and soon found herself participating in a neighborhood Bible study. Kayo also began reading the Bible on her own. She had many questions, since she knew very little about Christianity.

The Bible study members befriended Kayo. They asked her questions about her religious background and began to explain about Christianity. They listened to her explain her belief system. Gradually they earned Kayo's trust.

After attending the Bible study for several weeks, Kayo asked a profound question. She had heard members of the group say that Christ is the only way to salvation, so she asked, "Am I understanding you to believe that if my parents do not accept Christ as their Savior, they will go to hell?"

The Bible study leader hesitated for a moment. Kayo's question was not simply academic, but very personal. The leader was concerned that a truthful answer might drive Kayo away, but the leader also knew that she needed to speak the truth. She answered Kayo by explaining that God's plan of salvation was not something that the group members had invented, but that Christ himself had claimed to be the only way to heaven. She went on to say that ultimately God chooses those who will enter heaven; they can do so only through a trusting faith in Christ as Savior.

After the group read the relevant Scripture passages, Kayo said that this made sense to her. In fact, for the first time, she understood that Christianity was not simply one of many equally valid religions, but the only true way to God.

As you move through this lesson, your group members will learn that people listen to our message both through our actions as well as our words. Be aware that you may have an opportunity during this lesson to share the gospel with someone in your group who has not yet trusted Christ. Keep the door open and be alert to their words or body language. Offer to speak after the session to anyone who would like to talk more about following

Jesus. Say clearly that you want everyone in the group to understand the gospel message that sinners are saved only through faith in Jesus Christ.

The Appendix (p. 39) includes various gospel presentations. You will want to briefly review them with your group. Before you do, however, be sure that you are comfortable using one of those methods to share your faith. You may want to demonstrate to your group members how you would use one of those methods.

Optional Opening Share Question

Describe a situation when you had the right answer at just the right time. Have you ever had the right answer five minutes too late?

If you have any parents of teenagers in your group, this sharing time should be interesting. Group members may offer answers from work experiences or other family relationships.

1. *Colossians 4:5-6*

   ⁵Be wise in the way you act toward outsiders; make the most of every opportunity. ⁶Let your conversation be always full of grace, seasoned with salt, so that you may know how to answer everyone.

   a.   How would a person who is wise toward outsiders act?

Who are outsiders? Have you ever felt like an outsider? Most everyone has felt like an outsider at one time or another. In this passage, the apostle Paul is speaking of those who have not yet committed their lives to Christ. A person who is wise toward such people takes advantage of every opportunity to show them kindness. This person is well informed concerning the way others live and think, reacts to circumstances with clear thinking, and promotes good relations with others.

Why must believers be *wise* **toward outsiders?** In Paul's day Christians regularly suffered slanderous attacks from nonbelievers. It happens today too. Therefore Paul encourages believers to use wisdom in their lifestyle and speech in order to defuse any wrong impression nonbelievers may have about Christians. **How do you think Christians are to stay well informed about others? Does this require more than Bible knowledge? What impression might a well-informed friend have on an "outsider"?** Showing interest in others by asking sincere questions is usually appreciated. It also can provide an opening for presenting the gospel more clearly.

   b.   How is it possible to have the right answer for everyone's question?

Remember that God is the source of our message. God not only provides opportunities to share our faith but gives the words to say as well. That does not mean, of course, that we can forget about studying the Bible. As we delve into the Scriptures on a daily basis, God will provide "divine appointments" in which we will be able to share freely what we've been learning.

Some questions will stump us. We should acknowledge that fact and be willing to postpone an answer until after we've done more research. **Where do we look to find answers to difficult questions?** If you are leading a grow group, have members identify their favorite Bible study aids. You may want to recommend one or two commentaries or dictionaries that you have found helpful. Many Bible study aids are available on the Web at www.crosswalk.com. An excellent resource for personal use or to give to a questioning individual is *Hard Questions People Ask About the Christian Faith* by Case Van Kempen (Faith Alive, 2002, 1-800-333-8300).

Above all, don't be worried if you don't know the answer. It is OK to tell someone you'll look it up and respond later.

c. *Which is more important—the right answer or the right attitude? Or are they equally important?*

Having an appropriate attitude is a "must" when answering questions.
Sometimes your questioner may want only to derail you. But if you attempt to answer the questions in a loving and caring way you will have gained much relationally. Of course, we must try to be "right" on both levels. **Why do you think people respond more positively to right answers when we have a right attitude? What can help us from becoming negative and argumentative?**

2. *Acts 17:22-23*

> [22]Paul then stood up in the meeting of the Areopagus and said: "Men of Athens! I see that in every way you are very religious. [23]For as I walked around and looked carefully at your objects of worship, I even found an altar with this inscription: TO AN UNKNOWN GOD. Now what you worship as something unknown I am going to proclaim to you."

a. *Before what body of people does Paul speak in Athens? Why is this significant?*

The "meeting of the Areopagus" was a body of learned men who discussed old ideas and debated new ones. This court of philosophers formerly had met on the Areopagus (or Mars Hill), but now it met in the marketplace. The Athenians believed themselves to be some of the wisest people on earth, and so much of their time and energy was given to debating ideas and philosophies. Paul knew about this practice and took full advantage of it for the express purpose of sharing the message of Christ. **What can we learn from Paul's decision to engage the thinkers of his day on their turf? Where might you find similar settings today?** If you are leading a grow group, ask members to suggest ways they can directly engage the thinking of this world: write a letter to the editor of the local newspaper; engage in conversations on a chat room; take a stand for Christ in academic settings; run for political office or volunteer in a political campaign.

b.   *Do you think Paul was familiar with his audience? Explain.*

Paul used words, concepts, and even religious markers (altar to an unknown god) to indicate that he was aware of their philosophical and theological biases.

c.   *How did Paul gain the attention of his audience?*

Paul's speech was well reasoned and well presented. He said that he had "looked carefully" at their religious icons and he had made an effort to understand their view of God. He related to them on their level. **Why do you think this was an effective way to gain their attention? How do people feel when we talk about ideas that are important to them?** By "doing our homework" and asking people about their beliefs, we show a personal interest that establishes an important common ground with them.

3.   *Acts 17:24-28*

> [24]"The God who made the world and everything in it is the Lord of heaven and earth and does not live in temples built by hands. [25]And he is not served by human hands, as if he needed anything, because he himself gives all men life and breath and everything else. [26]From one man he made every nation of men, that they should inhabit the whole earth; and he determined the times set for them and the exact places where they should live. [27]God did this so that men would seek him and perhaps reach out for him and find him, though he is not far from each one of us. [28]'For in him we live and move and have our being.' As some of your own poets have said, 'We are his offspring.'"

a.   *Why do you think Paul quoted secular writers rather than Scripture?*

Paul's quotations from the Greek poets Epimenides and Aratus point to a question—what is the source of human life?—that is shared both by Paul and the Athenian thinkers. Of course, Paul's starting point is "the God who made the world and everything in it" (v. 24), but he takes care to maintain the interest of his listeners by quoting from their writers as well. They were able to understand and appreciate Paul's references. **Should we use secular sources to communicate God's truth today? Why or why not? How might we do that? What might be the danger?** It is important to note that Paul's quotations from the Greeks do not conflict with scriptural teaching. In turn, we should be very selective in our use of secular sources to back up our message. Those sources must clearly support the truth of God's Word.

b. *What can we learn from Paul's example?*

Paul's method of speaking with unbelievers should give us courage to do the same. Paul used Scripture as the basis of his message to the Athenians. We can do the same. We must be familiar with the Word and unwilling to compromise its truth.

In addition, Paul had thought through his speech. He started at the beginning—the creation of the world by God. (The beginning is always a good place to start!) His entire speech is well crafted and articulate. For us to think through our presentation of the gospel, to memorize key concepts and biblical themes, and to grasp the redemptive thread running through the entire Bible takes time and energy. But we must do it if our defense of the gospel is to be worth anything at all.

We've noted that using references to secular sources is a valid way to engage nonbelievers. Today we might refer to a familiar song lyric, movie, or author in order to meet someone on common ground. Many people are not familiar with the Bible. They can easily be put off by too many Bible verses. If secular references can help us convey spiritual truths, then they should be used with discretion.

4. *Acts 17:29-34*

²⁹"Therefore since we are God's offspring, we should not think that the divine being is like gold or silver or stone—an image made by man's design and skill. ³⁰In the past God overlooked such ignorance, but now he commands all people everywhere to repent. ³¹For he has set a day when he will judge the world with justice by the man he has appointed. He has given proof of this to all men by raising him from the dead."

³²When they heard about the resurrection of the dead, some of them sneered, but others said, "We want to hear you again on this subject." ³³At that, Paul left the Council. ³⁴A few men became followers of Paul and believed. Among them was Dionysius, a member of the Areopagus, also a woman named Damaris, and a number of others.

a. *What issue caused Paul's listeners to react (v. 32)?*

Most of Paul's listeners believed in the immortality of the soul, but this new teaching about the bodily resurrection of the dead gave them reason to reflect on what he said. Some of them rejected his speech, but others wanted to know more. They really did need to hear more about the subject. **Why must we be patient with people who are hearing Christian truths for the first time? What might we need to do in order to keep our listeners engaged?** There may be occasions when we must slow down in our presentation of the gospel, or we may have to repeat what we've said before. We should also take care not to use words or concepts that are completely foreign to our listeners. Their body language will provide important clues about how well we are communicating.

> b. *How did the Athenians react to Paul's speech?*

The Athenians reacted in three ways: belief, skepticism, and the desire to hear more. **Are these the most common responses people have when they hear the gospel for the first time?** Even the most convincing presentation of biblical truth will probably be met with one of these responses. **How should we feel when people reject our message? How can we know if our listener is rejecting the message or rejecting us?** Despite the rejection we will encounter (sometimes rejection of the message and sometimes rejection of the messenger), we must remember that people who do not believe today may yet come to faith tomorrow. **If you were hearing Paul's message for the first time, how might you react?**

5. *1 Corinthians 9:19-22*

> [19]Though I am free and belong to no man, I make myself a slave to everyone, to win as many as possible. [20]To the Jews I became like a Jew, to win the Jews. To those under the law I became like one under the law (though I myself am not under the law), so as to win those under the law. [21] To those not having the law I became like one not having the law (though I am not free from God's law but am under Christ's law), so as to win those not having the law. [22]To the weak I became weak, to win the weak. I have become all things to all men so that by all possible means I might save some.

> a. *How did Paul reach various groups of people?*

Paul reached people who were not like him because he took the time to acquaint himself with each group of people. Moreover, he identified with each group and spoke on their level. He believed that in order to effectively spread the gospel he had to relate to all people so that no one would be hindered from coming to faith. **Do you think Paul's approach compromised the truth? Was he being insincere?** Of course, the writer of Romans and many New Testament epistles cannot be accused of compromising the truth. Here Paul clearly states that his first allegiance is to the teachings of Christ (v. 21). It is in this context that Paul says he has "become all things to all men" (v. 22).

b. *What is the value of Paul's approach?*

Paul's approach as stated in verse 22 allows us to reach people at every level of society. We are not restricted to one or two classes of people or to people who live like us. **What does Paul assume about the nature of people? How should this assumption affect the way we view people?** Paul believed that all people have value. He was willing to identify with them in order to help them hear his message. This is the lesson for us today.

c. *What does this require of us?*

It requires us to study and understand people who are not like us in order to communicate on their level and to reach them with God's message of grace. We naturally gravitate toward people who share our ethnic background and economic lifestyle. Nevertheless, we have a responsibility to seek out people from other walks of life. **How might we do this?** Take a few minutes to make this discussion practical. Perhaps your church could sponsor a parenting class, an AA group, or a book discussion club. These would put you in contact with different groups of people. Help your group think of additional ways to connect with other types of people. If appropriate, you might want to pass these suggestions along to your church leaders.

6. *2 Corinthians 4:1-2a*

¹Therefore, since through God's mercy we have this ministry, we do not lose heart. ²ᵃRather, we have renounced secret and shameful ways; we do not use deception, nor do we distort the word of God.

a. *What kept Paul from losing heart?*

Paul indicates that his ministry has come about through God's mercy. This is what gives him encouragement. In other words, when God helps us see our need to come to faith in Jesus, we, in turn, want to tell others about the truth we have discovered. If God's mercy has touched us, we want to pass it on. If you are leading a grow group, ask, **How can we be more aware of God's mercy in our own lives? What difference does God's mercy make on a daily basis?**

b. *What did Paul renounce?*

Paul says that followers of Christ no longer do shameful things, no longer practice deception, and do not distort the Word of God. Finally, we do not give up on people by becoming discouraged. **What shameful things might Paul have in mind?** Paul is referring here to things that are done in secret. Commentator R. V. G. Tasker writes that a more accurate rendering is "disgraceful and underhanded ways," things that would be done by an unscrupulous politician or an ingratiating salesman *(2 Corinthians,* Eerdmans, 1982). **Why must these things not be done?** They would bring dishonor to Christ.

7. *2 Corinthians 4:2b-4*

> ²ᵇOn the contrary, by setting forth the truth plainly we commend ourselves to every man's conscience in the sight of God. ³And even if our gospel is veiled, it is veiled to those who are perishing. ⁴The god of this age has blinded the minds of unbelievers, so that they cannot see the light of the gospel of the glory of Christ, who is the image of God.

a. *How did Paul present the truth to people?*

Paul approached people with integrity of heart and purpose. He did not use trickery or deceit, nor did he distort biblical truth. In other words, he used the Scriptures correctly, not forcing them out of context in order to prove a point. Remember that God's mercy fueled Paul's ministry. **What does this suggest about why Paul was so eager to preach the gospel?**

b. *Who and what keep people from believing?*

Who is "the god of this age"? None other than Satan himself. He is the one who causes the gospel to be veiled to those who hear but choose to reject it. This veil blinds them to the truth. It covers their hearts and minds. There is no veil on the gospel, however; its message is clear. **How can this veil on unbelievers be lifted?** It can be lifted only by God, who "made his light shine in our hearts" (v. 6). Encourage group members to share how that veil has been lifted in their own experience or in the experience of someone they know.

Be sensitive to those in your group who may not have yet put their trust in Christ. Acknowledge that verse 4 is very plain concerning the role of Satan in unbelievers. Yet the good news is that on the cross Christ defeated the power of Satan. Those who come to Christ in faith will receive eternal life, and the spiritual blinders will be removed. This is the gospel. Offer again to meet individually with anyone in your group who has questions about these things.

c. *What is God's role and what is our role in convincing people regarding the truth of the gospel?*

We are merely the messengers; only God's Spirit convinces people regarding the truth. Even the most confused presentation of the gospel can produce positive results if we understand that it is ultimately God who does the convincing. If you are leading a grow group, ask, **Does this fact give us** permission to make a poor presentation? Does it take the pressure off? Explain.

8. *Summary*

What have you learned from Paul's example that will help you share your faith?

We cannot expect everyone to accept or even to listen to our message. (And we are in good company. Many people rejected the message of Christ from the lips of the apostle Paul.) We also may find it difficult to work up the courage to say anything. However, the more we speak with others, the easier it will become. It is important that we study the Bible and learn about people so that we can be ready to answer those who ask us about our faith. Nevertheless, we need to remember that God is the one who lifts the veil from the human heart.

As you conclude this lesson, refer group members to the Appendix (p. 39), where they will find several gospel presentations. Explain that these are not intended to be "canned" presentations. Instead, they are methods that group members might use when someone asks them about their faith. They should choose one and memorize it so they will be ready when God gives them an opportunity to share the gospel. There is also a list of conversation starters and ways to inquire whether people have come to faith. The "Turning Point" questions are another helpful tool. You may also indicate that if people are on the verge of coming to faith, they can pray a simple prayer using the words *yes, please,* and *thank you.* They can say, "Yes, I want to receive Christ. Please take away my sins. Thank you for dying on the cross."

On page 43 you'll find a suggested reading list. These books will help group members grow in their ability to articulate their faith. Encourage members to read one or two of them. Finally, challenge them to put into practice what they have learned in these four lessons. Sharing your faith and seeing others come to Jesus can bring incredible joy and pleases God.

Appendix
How to Share Your Faith

Once you have prayed, developed a passion for lost people, and gained a basic understanding of culture, begin to concentrate on the message. The number of evangelism techniques and approaches has exploded over the past fifty years. Use one that is natural and fits your personality. The last thing you want to do is sound like a salesperson giving a "canned" presentation.

Do Versus Done

One easy way to explain the basic gospel message is called "Do Versus Done." All other religions teach that a person has to *do* something to get into heaven. Christianity teaches a different way to heaven. It is not what we do, but what Jesus has already *done* by his sacrifice on the cross that gets us in. John 14:6 is a helpful passage to use.

The Roman Road

"The Roman Road" uses Romans 3:23; 6:23; and 10:13 to give the essential points of the gospel.

Not a Religion

You can also mention that Christianity is not a *religion;* it is a *relationship* with God through Jesus Christ. Use Ephesians 2:8-9 and tell how Christianity is a gift from God.

The Bridge

Evangelistic booklets such as *The Bridge* are useful. They give a basic gospel outline that is easy to understand. The "bridge" diagram (p. 40) can also be drawn on something as simple as a paper napkin in a restaurant if you do not have the booklet available.

The Way of Salvation—Romans 3:21-31

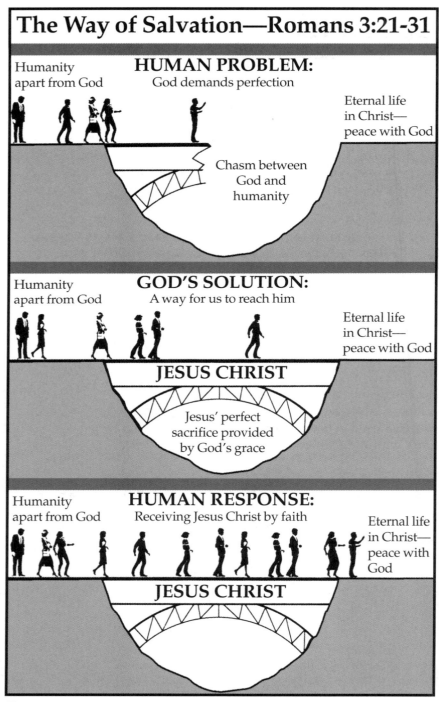

HUMAN PROBLEM:
God demands perfection

Humanity apart from God

Eternal life in Christ— peace with God

Chasm between God and humanity

GOD'S SOLUTION:
A way for us to reach him

Humanity apart from God

Eternal life in Christ— peace with God

JESUS CHRIST

Jesus' perfect sacrifice provided by God's grace

HUMAN RESPONSE:
Receiving Jesus Christ by faith

Humanity apart from God

Eternal life in Christ— peace with God

JESUS CHRIST

Regardless of the method you use, what is most important is that you express the basic message clearly and simply. Be sure to explain human sinfulness, the uniqueness of Christ, the meaning of his death and resurrection, and the need to trust in Christ for salvation. Moreover, it is best to memorize the presentation and supporting Bible verses. Then, when an opportunity arises, you'll be ready to speak with confidence.

Tell Your Own Story

Telling your own story of faith can be an effective way to share the gospel. The late Anthony Hoekema, who wrote extensively on the cults, said that our personal testimony is the one thing few people could argue against. It can be very compelling for a nonbeliever to hear you explain how God has worked in your life.

You might describe either good or difficult circumstances, depending on your own experience or the need of the person with whom you are speaking. For example, someone might tell you something positive about your marriage or your children. Turn that comment into an opportunity to say how your relationship with Christ has made a big difference in your family life. Or perhaps after an illness or the death of a loved one, you can express how God was with you through that experience. Remember, if you tell people about your spiritual journey, it is only natural to ask them about theirs.

Ask Questions

Questions are useful when talking about your faith experience. Ask people you talk with about their church background or some other nonthreatening topic. The more you know about their background or relationship with God, the easier it will be to relate to them. When they say something biblically incorrect or uninformed, respond with a phrase like "That's interesting." Then, if necessary, gently point out that Scripture gives a different perspective.

If your friend seems perplexed by your conversation, ask if what you are saying makes sense. If it doesn't, ask what is not clear. Remember that you will likely have an opportunity to speak with your friend again. Sharing the gospel can be done over a period of time while the Holy Spirit works in the person's life.

If your friend joins you at a Bible study or an outreach event at your church, be sure to get his or her reaction. For example, ask, "What did you learn about Jesus in our Bible study?" Or "What did you think about this evening's event? What was particularly meaningful?" Encouraging people to express an opinion makes communication easier. Be sure to be nonjudgmental. Let them know that you care about what they think even if you do not agree with their perspective.

The Turning Point

If you sense that someone is interested in Christianity, you can shift the focus from your message to the person's response in a natural and intentional way by asking what Bill Hybels calls "turning point questions" *(Becoming a Contagious Christian,* Zondervan, 1994, p. 184).

- What is preventing you from crossing the line of faith?
- What is preventing you from following Jesus?
- Have you come to the place where you think God could do a better job of running your life?

If the person is ready to accept Jesus as Savior, you can pray with him or her repeating the words after you. (You may need to explain that prayer is simply talking to God.) After you have prayed with the person, show your excitement for what has just occurred.

Express the importance of the step he or she has just taken. Encourage the person to continue to talk with God in prayer.

—Adapted from *So You've Been Asked to Share Your Faith,*
by Brent and Diane Averill (Faith Alive, 2001, 1-800-333-8300).

Recommended Reading

Averill, Brent and Diane. *So You've Been Asked to Share Your Faith.* Grand Rapids, Mich.: Faith Alive, 2001. 1-800-333-8300.

Gumbel, Nicky. *Searching Issues.* Colorado Springs: David C. Cook, 1996.

Hybels, Bill, and Mark Mittelberg. *Becoming a Contagious Christian.* Grand Rapids, Mich.: Zondervan, 1994.

Little, Paul. *How to Give Away Your Faith.* Downers Grove, Ill.: InterVarsity Press, 1972.

Mittelberg, Mark. *Building a Contagious Church.* Grand Rapids, Mich.: Zondervan, 2000.

Pippert, Rebecca Manley. *Out of the Saltshaker and into the World.* Downers Grove, Ill.: InterVarsity Press, 1999.

Strobel, Lee. *Inside the Mind of Unchurched Harry and Mary.* Grand Rapids, Mich.: Zondervan, 1993.

Evaluation Questionnaire

DISCOVER THE JOY OF SHARING JESUS

As you complete this study, please fill out this questionnaire to help us evaluate the effectiveness of our materials. Please be candid. Thank you.

1. Was this a home group ___ or a church-based ___ program? What church?

2. Was the study used for
   ___ a community evangelism group?
   ___ a community grow group?
   ___ a church Bible study group?

3. How would you rate the materials?

   Study Guide
   ___ excellent ___ very good ___ good ___ fair ___ poor

   Leader Guide
   ___ excellent ___ very good ___ good ___ fair ___ poor

4. What were the strengths?

5. What were the weaknesses?

6. What would you suggest to improve the material?

7. In general, what was the experience of your group?

Your name (optional) _____

Address _____

_____

8. Other comments:

(Please fold, tape, stamp, and mail. Thank you.)

Faith Alive Christian Resources
2850 Kalamazoo Ave. SE
Grand Rapids, MI 49560